Message of the Day

Written by: Annie L. Peters

Photos by: Joe Prible

Blessings 2 Good
P.O. Box 2811
Orland Park, IL 60462

Message of the Day
Text copyright 2011 by Blessings 2 Good, Inc.
Photo copyright 2011 by Joe Prible
Cover design 2011 by Susan Doctor

Library of Congress Control Number: 2011961656

Printed in the United States of America.
All rights reserved. No part of this book may be used or reproduced in any manner whatsoever without written permission except in the case of brief quotations embodied in critical articles and reviews.

Thank you to all who have encouraged, supported and helped me make the printing of this book possible.

Many Blessings and much Love to you!

If we continue to look at the things we don't have, we'll never be thankful for what we do have.

They say the eyes are the windows to the soul. Let your soul be filled with heavenly things simply by always looking up.

What if the only hope someone has is the hope you have for them?

Always have hope no matter what the circumstance – for you and each person who crosses your path – because ...

No one and nothing is hopeless.

If we want to live a life blessed with moments of "being in the right place at the right time", then we need to ensure our hearts are in the right place so we can hear the next step we are to take.

Ammie L. Peters

Just as silver has to be put to heat to remove the dross, our hearts have to be put to the fire to become pure.

There's an old saying that "if you can't take the heat, get out of the kitchen." But I say, no matter how hot it gets, stay in the kitchen!

Remember – silver does not go to the silversmith to be shaped into beautiful jewelry until it has withstood the heat, leaving only pure silver for shaping.

When we have the courage to step out of the nest ...

We discover we have wings to fly.

I Love You

You're Amazing!

> Sharing love can be as simple as a spoken word …
>
> Today and every day, let your words encourage, uplift or bring hope to another.

There's no one else like you

I'm thankful you're in my life!

I NEED YOU

A flower's beauty speaks for itself by simply being what it was made to be.

Live your life so that others see the beauty of who you were made to be.

Give and receive Love like an Angel ...

Ammie L. Peters

If people would learn how to truly love – how to give it and receive it – there would be no hurt in the world.

Learn to give and receive love unconditionally, striving to never hurt another through your actions or words.

Forgive ...

Forgiveness is a gift to both the forgiver and the one forgiven. If we learn to forgive the <u>person</u>, we are allowing God to work on changing their <u>actions</u>. Confusing the two holds us back from having true forgiveness within our hearts.

True Love is when the world shatters your heart and God gives you His.

Ammie L. Peters

Illustration by Lanetta Fox

Have you ever had someone walk into a room and their smile, their kindness ... their very heart inspired you because it changed the atmosphere of the room?

Be that person.

Just as a butterfly is meant to leave the cocoon, we go thru dark times to be transformed into something beautiful!

Imagine how silly a butterfly would look if it decided to carry that cocoon around (not to mention it would prevent it from flying) but yet we tend to hold on to that cocoon (those dark times ... mistakes we've made, horrible things that have happened to us in life). If we can't get past the cocoon, how do we ever expect to fly?

Learn from the dark times whether it is strengthening your faith or purifying your heart (meaning no longer make the same mistakes) ... then you will see a transformation you didn't think was possible.

Believe

Today is a NEW day, embrace it!

Ammie L. Peters

Every now and then we need reminded that every-day aboveground is a good day! So, when the world continues to throw dirt on you, shake it off, step up, and soon you will find yourself on top again … there IS a plan for you, don't let anyone convince you otherwise.

The difference between achievement and success is being heart focused ...

Ammie L. Peters

Achievement is led by the mind (i.e. we work hard to accomplish something). However, when success is led by the heart, we are passionate about what we do. Regardless of the results, we have a feeling of success that radiates through us because we love what we are doing. The true blessings come when our heart puts our mind to it.

Love what you do!

A smile can change someone's day.

Share yours … someone needs it today.

An important step towards being the person we were made to be is learning how to put others before ourselves. When we are stuck in the "I want", "I need", thinking then we become very selfish.

When we learn to remove "I" from selfish then the word speaks more clearly to our hearts. Here's what I mean, delete "I" from selfish and you get SELF__SH, which reads like this "self…shhhhhh".

So, the next time your mind starts down the "I" road, stop and remind yourself to shhhh that thought and listen to what you are really supposed to do - the clarity of what you begin to hear will amaze you.

We've all heard the saying "It's not what you say but how you say it". It IS what you say AND how you say it.

We need to be mindful not only of the words that we speak but the manner and tone in which they are spoken. Pay attention to how the words that people speak and the tone in which they use them impacts the way you feel. Positive and uplifting words bless when spoken.

Bless each person who crosses your path today.

Ammie L. Peters

You can't stop and smell the roses unless you take a moment to walk thru the garden first. Life is so busy that I think we often miss the garden all together.

A couple of years ago I flew to see my mom on Mother's Day. After a wonderful weekend we headed back to the airport. On the way, we decided to stop and have lunch at a small café in town. I made a wrong turn. As a result, we stumbled upon this truly amazing rose garden that had to be an acre big. It was tiered meaning there was about ¼ acre filled with roses, then you would step down a few steps and there was another ¼ acre and you kept going – it seemed endless. We were surrounded by the most amazing beauty I personally have ever experienced. The fragrance combined with the colors and natural beauty was truly captivating and brought peace to my soul that is hard to describe. The next time you make a wrong turn, don't get discouraged ... look for the rose garden.

Before a flower can grow into something beautiful, it finds itself covered in dirt. It's important to understand that not only is the dirt (i.e. our mistakes, bad decisions, lack of self-control) used to help us grow; it is used to help others grow as well.

There's a person in your life today where all you're seeing is the dirt. See past the dirt and have hope knowing a beautiful flower can and will bloom.

What if your love and your prayers are the very water God is sending to help that flower bloom, but you can't see past the dirt?

See past the dirt.

Life is a gift – unwrap it and look inside! Don't throw it away just because you don't like the wrapping paper. In life, we would never shove a gift aside refusing to open it because we didn't like the wrapping paper; but, we often do exactly that with each day we are given.

You woke up today – that means you've been given a gift ... a gift that was custom made just for you! Open it and look inside; don't let it go to waste.

In order to get the life you want …

Get into the life you have!

Years ago a contract was entered into with a handshake and a man's word.

Live your life so that when you extend your hand and give your word, the other person knows that your word means far more than any legal written contract because there is no fine print.

When you are faced with a difficult person (someone who is being inconsiderate, or is outright mean), are you able to remain the person you were called to be? When we react with the same negativity, we fuel the very fire that's burning us. Our first reaction should be to put the fire out with the water of patience and kindness, not to add more fire.

What gift (i.e. skill, talent) have you been given that you can share with others? There are so many people that need help but often the first approach is money focused (i.e. donations, fundraisers) in order to purchase whatever is needed.

But what if we take an opposite approach and each give of our gifts? The possibilities are endless!

I want to encourage you to take some time today to think about what skill you have been blessed with and who you can share it with - whether it is offering your services for free or coming to the side of someone as a mentor to pass on your trade.

Stars don't need the darkness to shine; the darkness just makes them stand out ...

Set yourself apart – shine bright!

The most important language we can speak comes from our heart. Let people hear who you are without a single word spoken from your lips.

When we look to a star filled night, our eyes immediately focus upon the light of the stars instead of the darkness that surrounds them. Learn to do this in all areas of your life.

Seek to have your eyes focus on the good so that even when surrounded by a blanket of darkness your eyes automatically look for the light.

Miracles surround us every day,
They knock upon our door.
So take the time to look for them,
And watch your blessings soar.

Ammie L. Peters

A friend of mine was facing a hard time in life and was struggling with believing God is real so a few of us took a walk on the beach. I began to share with her how God's Love is everywhere and I find hearts all around to remind me of that beautiful Love. I asked God to let us find some rocks shaped like hearts.

As we walked, it was amazing what happened. Each step we took we found rock after rock all shaped like hearts! It was a day we'll never forget.

We are truly surrounded by miracles every day but we have to look for them or we'll miss the blessing.

Don't miss the blessing.

Ammie L. Peters

When a mistake is made in life (whether it is by you or someone else), focus on the lesson to be learned and not the mistake that was made. If we focus on the mistake then we will miss the blessing of what we are to learn as a result of going through it. People do change and one of the biggest motivators for change is learning from mistakes. So if you make a mistake, learn from it and encourage others to as well so we no longer <u>miss</u> what we are to <u>take</u> away from mistake.

I saw the most beautiful sunrise not long ago. The sun was filled with vibrant colors of yellow, orange and pink. Its rays extended out as far as the eyes could see adding a touch of color to everything within its path. The clouds filling the sky surrounding it reflected the same beauty. It was as if the wind had carried the colors and gently dusted everything with a perfect amount of beauty, brightness and color.

Each morning we rise, we have an opportunity to paint everything that surrounds us … the color(s) we use on our paint brush is up to us.

Paint the world today with the beauty of who God created you to be letting your rays shine far and wide.

Every time you find a penny tails up, remind yourself to live the honesty that Abe Lincoln lived. He is an incredible example of how we need to live, and is a true inspiration to all. If more of us followed his example, this world would be filled with people who have the same integrity that he had.

Change can happen but it has to start with us first.

We all have different calls on our lives and we all have different gifts. Some people are great musicians, some great business people, some great Dads, some great doctors, some great listeners and some have a way of making someone feel good just by their smile.

If you are still breathing then you are meant to impact another human being! Don't ever underestimate that you are on this earth for a very specific purpose that only you can fulfill. How do you know that a kind word you spoke to someone wasn't the first kind word ever said to them so now they feel self-worth? Or maybe YOUR prayer is what God heard to save a life or bring a miracle?

You are important – believe it because it's true.

Take a moment – sit back, close your eyes and visualize a perfectly still lake. In the middle of this lake is a small island of beautiful green grass, wild flowers and a big Willow Tree in the center. The branches of the tree extend just past the edge of the island to gracefully rest over the water. A drop of water slowly rolls down from the very top branch, then down to a smaller branch then to a leaf. It then makes its way into the water. That single drop creates a perfect circle on the quiet, still lake. That circle then creates another circle, and that circle creates another until beautiful ripples extend all the way to the shore.

You are the drop of water, and each circle represents a person's life you can touch today. What you bring to that first ripple will impact each ripple after it. You have the potential of impacting many people by a single act of kindness and even reaching someone half way across the world before days end all by the ripple you start today.

We all have hearts that beat the same so see others for their heart and not the rhythm in which it beats.

Love one another.

Ammie L. Peters

Until we can trust ourselves, we can't fully trust at all. So the first step in learning how to trust is living a trustworthy life. Remember, it's never too late for you or anyone else.

If you've made mistakes, learn from them and leave them in the past.

Today is a new day for a reason, understand the depth of that gift and walk forward in it.

The only difference between morning and mourning is "u".

It's up to us how we welcome the new day. We can choose to walk around in sadness, regret, or sorrow about all that faces us in life. Or we can choose to embrace the day with thankfulness knowing that God is bigger than all the troubles we face and that there IS a plan for us.

No longer let your mind travel down the road of thoughts filled with regret, sorrow or unworthiness instead focus your mind on the good knowing today is a new day, a new beginning, and you woke up for a reason. When you begin to change your mind you will be amazed at how clearly you can hear what your heart is saying.

The only limits in your life are the boundaries your mind has set. Your mind cannot comprehend what God has planned for you – once you open up to that and believe it, you will see things begin to unfold in your life that you never could have imagined possible.

Ammie L. Peters

We often look right past beauty until our angle changes, allowing us to see the reflection of its hidden glory. (This picture is of morning dew that formed underneath a glass patio table.)

When something is going good in your life, don't allow fear to come in to try and tell you the other shoe will drop. Instead, be thankful for the other shoe because then both of your feet are equipped to get out there and walk the path you were called to walk.

Transform your mind and focus on the good ...

Fear nothing – be hopeful in everything.

When life comes at you and emotions began to rise up (like when people know the exact button to push), ask yourself is your reaction one of love, joy, peace, patience, kindness, goodness, faithfulness, gentleness and self-control? If the answer is no, then …

1) Don't react.
2) Hold your tongue.

For when we live a life of Love, Joy, Peace, Patience, Kindness, Goodness, Faithfulness, Gentleness and Self-control we discover the key to a fully blessed life.

Thank you for helping to bring love to the heart of another. A portion of each book sold is donated to In the Spirit of Love Foundation. We believe that when we desire to give, we have learned how to live. To encourage you to keep the love going, each purchase includes your very own Live it! Card. To receive your card, please email liveit@blessings2good.com. Ensure you include your name, address, order #, and place of purchase. Once received, register your card online at www.inthespiritoflove.org then do a random act of kindness/love and pass the card to the recipient encouraging them to do the same. Revisit the website. Enter what love you "lived". Periodically check back to track where the card has traveled and what love has followed. Ensure to request your card today so you can Live it!

Thank you for being a very important part of bringing much needed love to the world.

Many Blessings to you!

Made in the USA
Charleston, SC
20 December 2011